The Others Raisd in Me

150 Readings of Sonnet 150
a plunderverse project

by Gregory Betts

COPYRIGHT © 2009 Gregory Betts

ALL RIGHTS RESERVED. No part of this book may be reproduced or transmitted in any form or by any means whatsoever without written permission from the publisher, except by a reviewer, who may quote brief passages in a review. For information, write Pedlar Press at PO Box 26, Station P, Toronto Ontario M5S 2S6 Canada.

ACKNOWLEDGEMENTS
The publisher wishes to thank the Canada Council for the Arts and the Ontario Arts Council for their generous support of our publishing program.

Variants of 1, 2, 3, 7, 11, 12, 13, 14, 21, 22, 41, 51, 117 and 118 were previously published as a chapbook by Trainwreck Press.

LIBRARY AND ARCHIVES CANADA
CATALOGUING IN PUBLICATION

Betts, Gregory Brian, 1975-
    The others raisd [sic] in me / Gregory Betts.

Poems uncovered by crossing out words and letters in Shakespeare's Sonnet 150.

ISBN 978-1-897141-30-4

    I. Title.

PS8553.E852O85 2009   C811'.54   C2009-905885-5

DESIGN
Zab Design & Typography, Toronto

COVER PHOTO
courtesy Archives of Ontario

TYPEFACE
Garamond Premiere Pro, Adobe

Printed in Canada

The Others Raisd in Me

THIS BOOK, APPEARING exactly four hundred years after the publication of Shakespeare's infamous sonnets, creatively misreads his Sonnet 150 as a prophetic program for the centuries of Western culture from his time through to our future doom. The rise of modern individualism in the sixteenth century has provoked a rush of arts, science and technology; consecutive waves of idealistic revolutions that pushed humanity beyond the limits of the body. The mechanical evolution of the human experience builds from the "I" within us to its projection and animation in cybernetic form. The Others that rise are the self and its metal shadow.

Each line in the original poem predicts a chapter in this progression.

All of the poems in this book were uncovered by crossing out words or letters in William Shakespeare's Sonnet 150.

This work has to develop to the highest degree the art of citing without quotation marks. Its theory is intimately related to that of montage.
— WALTER BENJAMIN, *The Arcades Project* (1940)

Language takes on the thickness of a material or a *medium*.
— PAUL RICOEUR, *La Métaphore vive* (1975)

O from what powre hast thou this powrefull might
16

With insufficiency my heart to sway?
30

To make me give the lie to my true sight,
44

And swere that brightnesse doth not grace the day?
58

Whence hast thou this becomming of things il,
72

That in the very refuse of thy deeds
84

There is such strength and warrantise of skill
98

That in my minde thy worst all best exceeds?
112

Who taught thee how to make me love thee more
126

The more I heare and see just cause of hate
140

O though I love what others do abhor,
154

With others thou shouldst not abhor my state:
170

If thy unworthinesse raisd love in me
184

More worthy I to be belov'd of thee
198

To Ted, Michael, Stephen and Andrew
the brothers raisd with me

The Others Raisd in Me

O from what powre hast

thou this powrefull might

may I fear thy majesty, who alone art powerful
— ELIZABETH I, *Prayer 3* (1563)

Inquire what power and operation the difference
of the bodies
— FRANCIS BACON, *De Augmentis Scientiarum* (1623)

1. *ReadMe Doc*

what powre this we
in my art.

make me sigh
swere that
grace is of things.

in my mind –
how to make and see

the others
raisd in me.

2.

what is
missing
when this
becoming

thinks,

        exceeds

who taught
me to see
hidden

this word

3.

what is powre
when is strength a skill

who taught thee
how to make love

        more, more

what is *in* love
to belove

4.

give to my sight
every deed
that others do
to raise love
to be belov'd

5.

powreful
    lie

grace my cause
to be bed of thee

6.

from tongue
sight,
and words
touch;
rush
tonguewards
madly

7.

o
the more
i make love
the more
worthy i be

8.

a fullness
a moon
reached
thru me

9.

we are not
made of words
tho we is

10.

will we
ever me
again?

With insufficiency

my heart to sway?

> The pain was so severe that it made me utter several moans. The sweetness caused by this intense pain is so extreme that one cannot possibly wish it to cease.
> — TERESA OF AVILA, *Of Visions* (1565)

> thee hast yet left me the knees of my heart
> — JOHN DONNE, *Prayer* (1624)

11.

simile as
a brightness
like a smile

12.

from a smile in
that brightness of winter
i hear a snow in me

13.

as i fight
with insufficiency

my art sways
to give the lie

to grace
and reason

14.

from what haste
might i fit
my rust?

i age, old,
caught
with the –

should not;
did

15.

make me lie
swere

bright
becomes ill

my worst
exceeds hate

abhor abhor
my unworthiness

raise me
to be bled

16.

has this insufficiency
    strength
   to state
 unworthiness?

17.

was
i
raisd
in myth?

or
the letter
i

18.

there is no
discounted
letter

19.

O, Powre,
Light within,
Give the line
Grace to kill
my Mind.

Make these
   Veins
teethe.

20.

From what past might
my heart sway
to give to sight
a night grey?

When this coming of things
hints of deeds,
the rush to kill
my mind exceeds.

Ought the hate,
or the sea of hate,
though I wash
it, the rot not abate:

if wor is in me
I bleed of thee.

To make me give the

lie to my true sight,

acting, may, by an appropriation that disguises
its true sense, serve a little to palliate the absurdity
— JOHN LOCKE, *An Essay Concerning
Human Understanding* (1689)

Oh let not luxury's fantastic charms
Thus give the lie to your heroic arms;
Nor for the ornaments of life embrace
Dishonest lessons from that vaunting race
— JOHN MILTON, *The Remonstrance
of Shakespear* (1749)

21.

might
make me

my mind
make
me more

more my
me more

22.

my heart
my ear
my mind

i hear, see,
love

my state,
me, i

23.

i swear
that in my mind
voices
lie

24.

who's there?
who?
who's there?

25.

i inks
methinks

26.

plunder that
delusion that
solution as
the
world

27.

letters are oracles

like miracles

28. *Of Love*

she said
he said
shed

29. *Swan Song*

startle
me
immortal

30.

cut from marble
i find words for
      d
  a
     v
    i
    d

And swere that brightness

doth not grace the day

That which is good for the head, is evil for the neck and shoulders
— JAMES I, *A Counter-Blaste to Tobacco* (1604)

Liberty is doing whatsoever the Laws allow
— CATHERINE THE GREAT, *New Law Code* (1767)

31.

spring
winter
fall
summer

the order
undid

32.

oh from innocence

a becoming of things ill:

in my mind

love grows thin

33.

from a poet:

whisky is a
dangerous
siren tune

34.

nothing
is more
beautiful

35. *For Sandra Stephenson*

perchance
after
absence
 is

36. Other Plunders, or Criticism as Palimpsest

writing on
writing
   adding
   nothing

37.

when i say
me
i mean
how i made it
here

a metonymy
of thee

38.

after us
is coming

stateless

39.

from this powrefull wor

a blindness
of hate
of love

40. *Bacchus and Arquebus*

revelutionary
revolver

Whence hast thou this

I am becoming daily more and more alive to the delay
— RENÉ DESCARTES, *Discourse on the Method of Rightly Conducting One's Reason and of Seeking Truth in the Sciences* (1637)

the nature of things is such, that if abuses be not remedied, they will certainly increase, nor ever stop
— JONATHON SWIFT, *A Project for the Advancement of Religion and the Reformation of Manners* (1709)

becomming of things il,

> It must be something more than humour or accident that could occasion a custom so constant and universal as this, which has obtained in all ages and nations of the world, and amongst all ranks of men, the learned as well as the illiterate.
> — GEORGE BERKELEY, *A New Theory of Vision* (1732)

41.

what has
sway
has

warts and all

42.

powre powrefull
right brightness
ran rant
in mind

or more

or worthy

be belov'd

43.

his wit
in art
to make light
of that fuse
of strength and skill –

how he thought
Others should
rise to he

44.

Hamlet: My true sight
wears no grey
though colour
hears just cause;
of hate blind in
me my love.

45.

Ophelia: Swere that
do not stay
will indeed
move thee
else lose
my love.

46.

Hamlet: *Get thee to a nunnery!*

47.

Ophelia: I do not grace the day
for such straw rants.
That I blow with thou
should thus I die?

48.

MacBeth: Ah, bank no trust in him. Truth is rue and wrath.

49.

ho
no
ri
fi
ca
bi
li
tu
din
it...

50.

love's
labour's
cost

That in the very

refuse of thy deeds

the ill-success of Shakspeare's imitators produces no other effect, than to make him be considered as inimitable
— VOLTAIRE, *Letter on England* (1731)

To claim that there are objects on which reason should not be consulted, is to say that in the most important affairs, we must consult but imagination, or act by chance.
— JEAN MESLIER, *Superstition In All Ages* (1732)

I could form to myself an idea, I had in my arms a species of a monster, the refuse of nature, of men and of love.
— JEAN JACQUES ROUSSEAU, *Confessions* (1770)

51.

o	might
with	sway
to	sight
and	the day
when	il
that	deeds
there	skill
that	exceeds
who	more
the	hate?
o	abhor
with	my state
if	in me
more	of thee

52.

```
    w                   i
        l
                            l
    i
                    a
        m                   s
    h a   ke
          s
```

53.

```
p               e
                        a
                            re's
s               o       n
  ne   t                s
      refuse
   c                    l
                  o  s
u                          re
```

54. *Down the Aisle*

hast
my heart
the lie
doth
this becomming
very refuse
strength and
thy

to make
and see
love what
shouldst not
raisd
to be

55. Progressive Vowel Charts: A

56. Progressive Vowel Charts: E

57. Progressive Vowel Charts: I

58. Progressive Vowel Charts: O

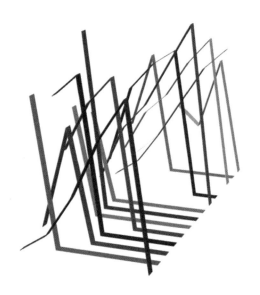

59. Progressive Vowel Charts: U

60. Progressive Vowel Charts: Y

There is such strength

But these selfish merchants were ambitious of the favour of being the last devoured; and the deficiency of art was supplied by the strength of obedient myriads.

— EDWARD GIBBON, *The History of The Decline and Fall of the Roman Empire* (1776)

and warrantise of skill

> We find, too, that those who are engaged in metaphysical pursuits are far from being able to agree among themselves, but that, on the contrary, this science appears to furnish an arena specially adapted for the display of skill or the exercise of strength in mock-contests – a field in which no combatant ever yet succeeded in gaining an inch of ground, in which, at least, no victory was ever yet crowned with permanent possession.
> — IMMANUEL KANT, *The Critique of Pure Reason* (1787)

61.

We
meet in arenas
that
fuse us
into
words

62.

speak
the myth

say
mackinaw

say
holy

63.

from
sport in ice
a grace that

thaws
immortalities

64.

from thin
ice
a loonie

is
scratching at
madness

65.

only
heroes
breakaway

66.

hockey
is better

in the
nude

67.

thus
puck bunny
trusts
just lust

68.

we own
the game
we sold

69.

hockey fans
over   distance
overtime

70. *In the United States and Newfoundland*

hockey
fight
in
Kandahar

That in my mind thy

From Earth the highest raptures and the best,
And all the Near and Far that he desireth
Fails to subdue the tumult of his breast
— JOHANN WOLFGANG VON GOETHE,
Faust (1806)

worst all best exceeds?

I, an outcast, with none to lead or drive me forward, paused. The old began to point at me as an example, the young to wonder at me as a being distinct from themselves; I hated them, and began, last and worst degradation, to hate myself. I clung to my ferocious habits, yet half despised them; I continued my war against civilization, and yet entertained a wish to belong to it.
— MARY SHELLEY, *The Last Man* (1826)

71. *A Peeling*

what power this
cinnamon sky

rust
sun-rinsed
in red

72. *Escape Meant*

perchance
reason
falls
by
its raisd limit

73. The Gamble of Love

feel to felt
all to all in
more worthy to be

74.

rustling sheets
grace the day

bird's songs
in afternoon heat

75.

this might be
the worst best
line ever
to be both

76.

superlative lies:

        best
exceeds more

77.

a green

brush over

the dust of

seasons

78.

my you recall
my we retell

79.

love thee
love what?

in love
love thee

80.

o o oe   o oe ll
    e e   o
o e e ve e l e o e
  e e e e o o e e
e e   o   e o   o l
  e ve e e o ee
e e   e   e o ll
    o ll e e ee
o   ee o o e love ee o e
e oe e   ee e o e
o o love   o e   o e   oe o
  o e o   o l o   o   e
  o e   e love e
 o e o   o e e belov'd o ee

Who taught thee how to

make me love thee more

There is something in the cause and consequence of America that has drawn on her the attention of all mankind. The world has seen her brave. Her love of liberty; her ardour in supporting it; the justice of her claims, and the constancy of her fortitude have won her the esteem of Europe, and attached to her interest the first power in that country.
— THOMAS PAINE, *The Crisis* (1780)

if thee wilt walk with me, I'll show thee a better
— BENJAMIN FRANKLIN, *The Autobiography of Benjamin Franklin* (1790)

81.

this might sway me,
this thing
in the very
war of my mind
exceeds
who taught me –

the more i hear and see it
no more
i be lov'd

82.

what power
wrote the lie
that rights
do fall to?

83.

if worth is raisd
more worth to love

84.

sway me to sigh
that right grace
this deed

and kill in my mind
all that won't shelter
my fear

85.

powre corrodes
by brute
hate

86.

outside
ideology
only teeth

87.

there is
no love
of nothing

88.

a win
a wind
a window

all staind
of hate

89. *To Lay Me Down*

lie still
till lies
lister

90.

we make love
out of nothing
evolve

The more I heare and

see just cause of hate

While fortunate drinkers know they can be conquered,
Hatred is condemned to this lamentable fate,
That she can never fall asleep beneath the table.
— CHARLES BAUDELAIRE, *Le Tonneau de la Haine* (1857)

We are not justified.
— OSCAR WILDE, *The Rise of Historical Criticism* (1905)

91.

From this
to that
when this
be that
there is
and is
that to hear

though what
i abhor
is more.

92.

of power might
brightness
do things ill

the very refuse
in my mind
taught me
the just cause
of hate.

93.

from
a press

power
with ink

steal
minds

from
the stole

94. *On Boomers*

pursue work
in worklessness

95.

for what it's worth
is made of earth

96.

might that
smell of malls
exchange
with others
soil?

97.

mail
order
border

98. *For Susan Rudy*

wage less economy

99.

the economic strength
of the economy state
rinsed in blood

100. *Equals*

you and i
math
identical
deviance

O though I love what

From childhood's hour I have not been
As others were—I have not seen
As others saw—I could not bring
My passions from a common spring—
From the same source I have not taken
My sorrow—I could not awaken
My heart to joy at the same tone—
And all I loved—I loved alone

— EDGAR ALLEN POE, *Alone* (1829)

others do abhor,

> We dread anarchy, and we abhor massacre and plunder.
> — ARTHUR YOUNG, *The Example of France* (1793)

> I shall not be everlastingly unhappy, and that's what frightens me.
> — STEPHANE MALLARMÉ, *Letter to Cazalis* (1863)

101. *I Dos: A Love Poem*

```
        O   I
  +     O   I
  ─────────────
            I
```

102. *To Be Of*

my to to me to
my of il in of
is of in my to
me of do my if
in me to be of

103. *Thy All*

the lie and not
the day
the thy and thy
all who how
the and see doe
not thy

104. *Give True That Doth Hast This*

from what hast thou this
with sway make give true
that doth hast thou this
that very such that best
thee make love thee more
more just hate love what
with thou love more thee

105.

powre might
heart sight

swere grace
deeds there
skill minde
worst heare

cause abhor
abhor state raisd

106.

whence things refuse

taught though others

others worthy belov'd

107. *The Seventh Power*

exceeds

108. *With Great Powre Comes Great Responsibility*

strength
shouldst

109. *I love him who laboureth
and inventeth*

powrefull
becomming

110.

insufficiency
brightnesse
warrantise
unworthinesse

111. *Veiled Endings*

at   as is full
in art   he   rue sigh
                            ERE

at   rightness do
                      race he
                      hence
          as his

                            coming

                    in
AT   he   fuse
             ere I ran   KILL

```
at      in                    or
            he                ore ore
                              ear      use


ATE           at he do       or it he
should no     or      ate worthiness
                      is              ORE
              or thy  lov'd
```

With others thou shouldst

not abhor my state

All along the tendency to deplore the absence of more has not been authorised. It comes to mean that with burning there is that pleasant state of stupefication.
— GERTRUDE STEIN, *Tender Buttons* (1914)

He only uses these accents for his familiars; with the others he is on the edge of paradox, pamphleteering, indeed of abuse.
— T.S. ELIOT, *Ezra Pound, His Metric and Poetry* (1917)

111.

is might within
sin?
it lights bright
things

thin in skill
i mist
i tilt with
wind mild

112.

Frame my
symmetry

tiger, tiger

regulate
my shame

113. *After the Internet*

the Cage stage
unravels

114.

```
e  v  o  l
  devol
  loved
l  o  v  e
```

115.

is love
in the body
is it
the shadow

116. *Plunderphonia*

a blank
returns the word

insert delete

117. *For Bök*

how
to how to
do north of
to stroll to
howl

how to
hold worth

to loot

118. *For Aaron Giovannone*

silencio
silencio

a void state
a void

119. *Pour Ubu, shithead*

science already
imagined this
solution

120.

perchance

a human
document

leaves

If thy unworthinesse

the literary phenomenon itself, which, raised to the status of the sacred, is severed from its specificity. Death thus keeps in our contemporary universe.
— JULIE KRISTEVA, *Approaching Abjection* (1982)

raisd love in me

> Silence can indicate my incompetence to hear, the lack of any event or relevant information to recount, the unworthiness of the witness, or a combination of these.
> — JEAN-FRANCOIS LYOTARD, *The Differend* (1992)

> What illustrates a transferred love onto language more than the fragmentary accumulations of privileged citations in which '[t]he word comes to carry its own ontology, its own reward for being'?
> — STEVE MCCAFFERY, *Prior to Meaning* (2001)

121.

o
to
oo

too

122.

ships:
> hate
> friend
> court
> love
>
> wor

123.

proof?
no.

but i
swear i
hear
others

124.

love
is the shortest
distance
between

125.

shortest
between three
is sex

126.

this is not
all we are

we evolve
with Others

127.

to evolve
machines
use
the word

128. *Modernism is a Word*

thee to Ms.
whence to once
hast to haste
I to as if

129. *Postmodernism is a Word*

Ms. to mist
once to never
haste to waste
as if to raisd in if

130. *After Words*

mist to math
never to now
waste to DNA
if to of

More worthy I to

> We have been awakened
> from our beds of crystal,
> and we have been invested
> by these bands of metal.
> — PAUL VALÉRY,
> *Le Cantique des Colonne* (1922)

be belov'd of thee

Human beings, like any other component or subsystem, must be localized in a system architecture whose basic modes of operation are probabilistic, statistical. No objects, spaces, or bodies are sacred in themselves.
— DONNA HARAWAY, *A Cyborg Manifesto* (1991)

If there is ego anywhere in this rhizome, it is a minor moment, a switching node between possible threads.
— DARREN WERSHLER-HENRY, *Noise in the Channel, or I Really Don't Have Any Paper: an antifesto* (2000)

131.

a new act
begins
in the rushed click
after math

132.

Fatal lies, tight and bright
this becoming of things
that refuse us

and of my mind
the metal
veers forward

133.

o from what powre
this art to kill

this is a
a war to kill
hating, hate
rinsed of life

134.

art transcends
of mind taught
metal minds

135.

Still Shatner
smiles
into the future

136.

What powre is
science art giving?

No beast.
No centre.
No blood.

137.

press
powre on
machines

138.

perchance
 machines
are
 de myth

139. *After the Revolution*

A Sign:

NO
returns

140. *Turn, turn, their turn*

for this
end to humanity

there is a season

141.

towns
names
gods
gone

machin(=e=)raisd

142.

cyborgs are
finally
irreducible

143. *Romanticism 1978-2008*

O frack Gods
Adama,
the very refuge of
ill minds:

Thrace sought
to love thee more;

Adama,
thy worthiness is
worthy to be lov'd.

144.

people say "yahoo"
when they destroy
one of the infinite

145. *Vows*

we (i/you)
see the edge of
forevermorrow

146. *Undercoverother*

OO from the

agentsy

oflanguage

147. Another dandy sign

no close
after closure

148. *A Thought, or The New Hyperion*

i am
is
negated by
this
negative ability

149.

at the end of things
strength of skin
exceeds

love of metal

150.

the end
of everything
isn't much

CHARLES EARL

BOOKS

If Language

Haikube (with Matt Donovan and Hallie Siegel)

EDITIONS

The Wrong World: Selected Stories and Essays of Bertram Brooker

In the Ward: Lawren Harris' Urban Poetry and Paintings

After Exile: A Raymond Knister Poetry Reader

GREGORY BETTS

is a poet, editor, critic and teacher. He lives in St. Catharines where he teaches at Brock University.
http://epc.buffalo.edu/authors/betts/